D1476266

# This Book Belongs To

●●●●●●●●●●●●●●●●●●●●●●●●●●●●●●●●●●●●●

# How To Use This Book

1. Start with any page that you like. Pick one that grabs you and gives you great ideas.
2. Look at the picture carefully.
3. Who and what is in the picture
4. What is happening?
5. Where is the story set? Indoors or outdoors?
6. Answer the questions and fill in the boxes.
7. Write your own story about the picture.
8. Color in the picture.

# Have fun & Let Your Imagination run wild!

What are these children doing?

Where is this taking place? A forest? beach?

# Write a story about the children

Why has this girl been digging?

What has she found?

# Write a story about treasure hunting

**Who lives in this castle?**

**Why does the castle need high walls?**

# Use your ideas to write a story

What time of the year is this?

# Write a story about Halloween

**What is he painting?**

**Who will he give the picture to?**

# Write a story about a painting

Is the lamp magic?

What happens when you rub the lamp?

# use your ideas to write a story

Why is the cat chasing the duck?

# Write a story about a chase

# What is the snowman wearing?

# Write about building a snowman?

What toppings are on the pizza?

Who is going to eat the pizza?

# How would you make a pizza?

**What is in the pot?**

**What happens when everything is cooked?**

# Write about a witch making a spell

# Where is the rocket going?

# Who or what is inside the rocket?

# Write a story about an astronaut

**Which weather do you like best?**

**What do you like to do in this weather?**

# use your ideas to write a story

# What is her dream about?

# Use your ideas to write about a dream

**What can the bird see?**

**Where will the bird fly to next?**

# Write a story about a bird

**What food do you love?**

**Do you like to eat alone or with others?**

# Describe a delicious meal you've eaten

What time of the year is this?

Do you like to play in the leaves?

# Write a story about Autumn

**What animal is this?**

**What do you think foxes enjoy doing?**

# Write a story about a fox

What can they see from the plane window?

# Write a story about a plane trip

What animal is this?

What happens when the eggs hatch?

# Write a story about baby birds

How are these children having fun?

# Write a story about ice skating

# This is a magic carpet

## Where will the magic carpet take you?

# Imagine flying on a magic carpet

Name three things you love about the natural word

Do you prefer mountains or beaches?

# Write a story about exploring

Is this gingerbread house large or small?

Could you live in this house?

# Write a story about your ideas

Where is the girl going?

What does it feel like to be on the water?

# Write a story about being in a boat

Is the tiger sad or happy?

Does the tiger live in the zoo or in a jungle?

# Write about the life of the tiger

## Who is going to ride in the sleigh?

## Where are they going?

# Write a story about what happens next

Is the alien friendly?

Where has the alien come from?

# Write about an alien or spacecraft

# Write three words to describe a magic spell

# Use your words to write a magic spell

## What animal is this?

## Where do penguins live?

# Write a story about a penguin and snow

Who is in the car?

Where are they going?

# Write a story about a trip in a car

Who is sailing on the ship?

Are the waves calm or rough?

# Write about a ship on the ocean

What is happening in the picture?

# Write a story about Christmas morning

Make a list of what is in the case.

# Write a story about a journey

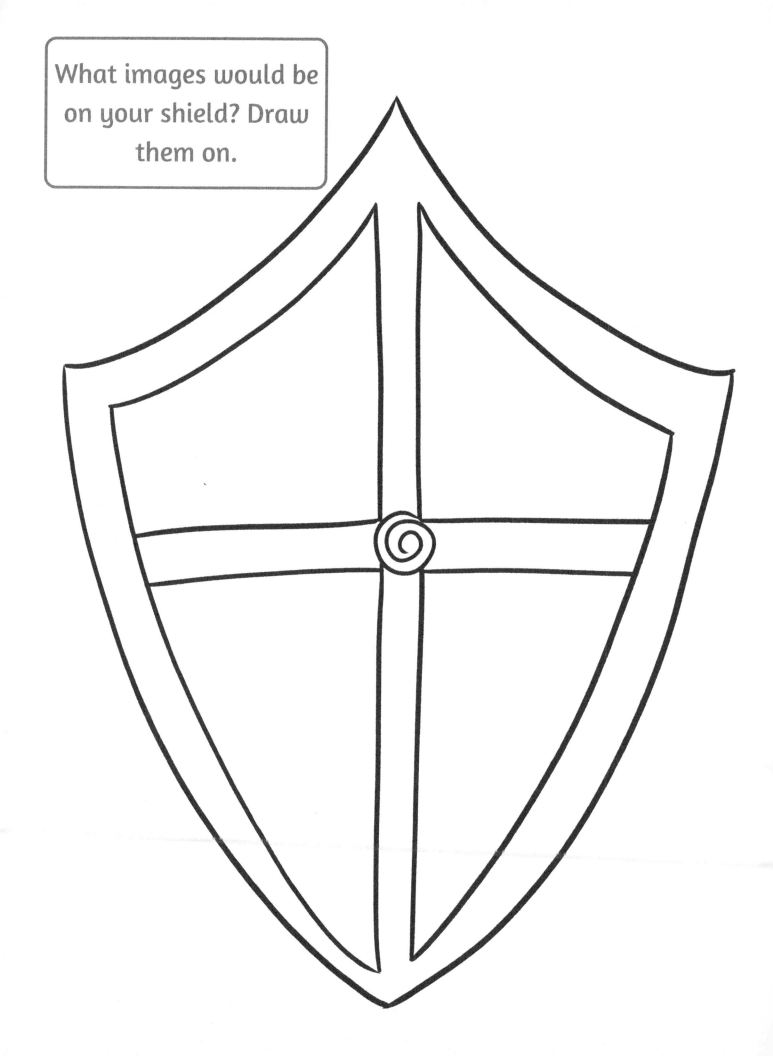

What images would be on your shield? Draw them on.

# Where would you use your shield?

# What is the boy drawing in his picture?

# use your ideas to write a story

## Who lives in this castle?

## How do they keep warm?

# Write a story about living in a cold place

What is the boy carrying?

What is he going to do?

# Write a story about a beach

Is it morning or night time?

Why is the boy in bed?

# Write a story about the boy in the bed

Where is the plane going?

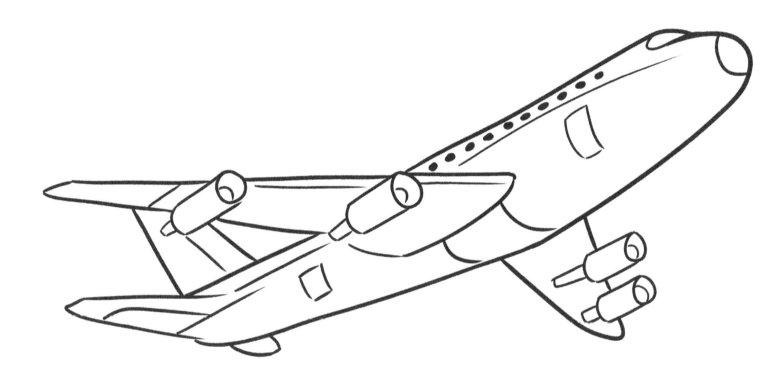

Who is on board the plane?

# Write a story about your ideas

Where does the mermaid live?

Who are the mermaid's friends?

# Write a story about a mermaid

Where are these children dancing?

Is it a special day?

# Write a story about a party

What animal lives in the tree?

How do they find food to eat?

# Write about the tree and an animal

What is he putting into his backpack?

# Write about a walk with a backpack

When does the witch fly on her broomstick?

Where does the witch go?

# Write a story about a witch

Is the dragon friendly?

What do you think dragons eat?

# Write a story about a pet dragon

# What can you see from a train window?

# Write a story about a train trip

What is in the drink? Is it nice or nasty?

Who is going to have the drink?

# Write a story using your ideas

What are they looking at?

Where are they going?

# Write a story about a magic map

**What is the girl pointing at?**

**Who is helping her?**

# Write a story about a pirate and a fight

Make a list of things you can do in the Summer

# Write a story about Summer fun

Made in the USA
Monee, IL
19 August 2020